AND YOU ARE THE ENTIRE POEM

Poetry and Translation

of

Fethi Sassi

Scarlet Leaf

2017

AND YOU ARE THE ENTIRE POEM

SASSI FETHI

© 2017 by Scarlet Leaf

All rights reserved. No part of this book may be reproduced, stored in a retrieval system or transmitted in any form or by any means without the prior written permission of the publishers, except by a reviewer who may quote brief passages in a review to be printed in a newspaper, magazine or journal.

Scarlet Leaf has allowed this work to remain exactly as the author intended.

ISBN: 978-1-988397-67-2

PUBLISHED BY SCARLET LEAF

Toronto, Canada

AND YOU ARE THE ENTIRE POEM

SASSI FETHI

Dedications

Do you know "Videros" What makes the writing marvelous

It is that is resembles painting tremendously?

Socrates to" Videros" in "The Conversations "

AND YOU ARE THE ENTIRE POEM

To the soul that paints the horizon

To the colors that used to dwell there

Uttering your eternal voice in languages

… … … … … …

Fethi

SASSI FETHI

FOR HER... UNIQUELY

And I am still loving you…

as if you were the next poem.

AND YOU ARE THE ENTIRE POEM

ASCENT OF HER DESIRE

She was travelling by night

in the twilight jubbah;

crying behind the cloud ascent of her

desire asking….:

who took away her harlot night?

SASSI FETHI

SUNSET

I have seen her….

running behind anemone sunset;

then she disappeared

AND YOU ARE THE ENTIRE POEM

EPITAPH

The shadows who stand up on her epitaph,

were reading the opening,

for the angels' argil.

SASSI FETHI

IDEA

I have found her between your lips;

cleaning as a star,

then it falls and disappears between words.

AND YOU ARE THE ENTIRE POEM

QUESTIONS MEMORY

This day is infatuated;

but the clockwise strung memory,

when the moments leave to search for

themselves…

SASSI FETHI

PROVOCATION

Ever since creation, the moon has been provoking all of the stars, to drag them down to depravity ....

AND YOU ARE THE ENTIRE POEM

THE SKY'S LIPS

The morning is kissing the sky's lips,

but the night…

has forgotten his cane hanging.

SASSI FETHI

THE DYNASTY OF WIND

You are descendent from the tempest,

whenever the wind groans on your cheek,

you stream like a poem...

A ROSE

Extravagant in its fragrance,

It said:

I used live in a rose…

SASSI FETHI

EMBRACE ME

Embrace me …

to keep me from starting to fall.

AN APOLOGY

I rub the scent of the fragrance;

I apologize to its charm,

but on the edge of the sleep, I retire with a rose…

SASSI FETHI

AT THE PRESENCE OF SATAN

At dawn…

at the presence of the Satan,

I kissed her,

and the poem erupted.

AND YOU ARE THE ENTIRE POEM

A SIN

On the navel of distance,

the ascent of sin escapes,

to expel the Goddess of temptation…

SASSI FETHI

A CHASE

At the temple of wind…

the night rejoices the pleasure of the fall,

and chases all the senses to dwell her eyes…

AND YOU ARE THE ENTIRE POEM

A BUTTERFLY

She flies as the water butterfly…

and flees the dream with no wings.

SASSI FETHI

IN THE ASCENT

At Sunset;

the twilight is being piled up at the ascent,

so that the stars could adorn themselves…

BREATHS

With the first beams of sunrise;

the night gave its last breaths…

and left a testament for the next morning.

SASSI FETHI

SO SHE IS

So she is…

when I like her;

I flow with poetry.

LONELY

I never paid attention,

my finger was lonely amongst the night's finger tips.

SASSI FETHI

THE TIME GALLOWS

The night is still hanging;

from the time gallows…

and never returned to bed…

AND YOU ARE THE ENTIRE POEM

STRANGE

The cloud had a thirsty…

It drank a star…

SASSI FETHI

WITH COFFEE

Every morning, I pick a quarrel with my coffee,

awaiting tender smile…

so that the coffee beans bloom with passion.

AND YOU ARE THE ENTIRE POEM

THE COVER OF DARKNESS

Of course…

I will wake up the night from its rainbow dreams;
to travel together into a spike,

the morning is still in the distance tumbler, folded
in the cover of darkness

SASSI FETHI

READER OF THE GRASS

He departs while doodling his blood,

extravagant in courting the sea…

and from the clouds' cracks is reading the grass,

hanging in the tree of the dusk.

AND YOU ARE THE ENTIRE POEM

THE POT OF THE TWILIGHT

Your night is my bouquet of waiting;

the sky is the pot of the twilight,

and I am…

flirting this evening dropping-down,

on your lips.

SASSI FETHI

DECREPITUDE

The night has shut its eyes,

and tottered to the Will…

AND YOU ARE THE ENTIRE POEM

THE LIGHTNING CHILD

After the last lines of rain…

all of the stars encounter each other at the ascent of the sky,

to brawl with the lightning child.

SASSI FETHI

THE MISTAKES OF THE RAIN

I am there…

filling up my suitcase with wind coughs,

to justify the rain's mistakes.

AND YOU ARE THE ENTIRE POEM

TRAITOROUS

Embroidered with instants, it is deceiving,

the trembles of the water;

to run all over in the wounds of distance.

SASSI FETHI

THE BREATHS OF THE NIGHT

She travels with her whoop,

to hold.

the night breaths.

AND YOU ARE THE ENTIRE POEM

SADNESS

Don' t leave me…

on your face,

I see all what I need of sadness.

SASSI FETHI

SUNSET PHOBIA

A phobia from sunset dwells inside of you,

and from the night's temptations…

the obscurity is falling down.

AND YOU ARE THE ENTIRE POEM

STEALTH

In the New Year's Eve,

troops of stars are lining up;

to enter the bars of the galaxy…

SASSI FETHI

THE TIDE

On the beach,

a fish is standing astonished,

listening to the story of tidal flows.

POTENTIAL PASSION

The rain ticks on the glasses of the story,

was nothing but…

a "Haiku " poem for a potential passion.

SASSI FETHI

THE ABSENCE

On the blank…

the absence packs its suitcase,

when the night asks for permission to enter.

AND YOU ARE THE ENTIRE POEM

A WHOOP'S DISTANCE

Between the blank and your lips,

there is a distance of a star…

on its palm a whoop.

SASSI FETHI

A COURTING

Just…

If the storm intended my courting;

and with the poetry yarns covered my chatter face,

to bring back the earth its first quorum…

and dedicate the cloud its beautiful names.

NEVER MIND

Never mind…

I will stay in that beautiful corner, lonely with my thoughts, certainly, the poems will cry the absence.

SASSI FETHI

IN THE WORDS' AVENUE

We weren't alone in the words' avenue,

we were about to write on the line;

but for the turmoil of the questions,

confusion path of labyrinth…

AND YOU ARE THE ENTIRE POEM

A THREAD

Strangulated in my loneness,

I search for an invisible thread to tie,

my death to my poetry…

to breathe my poem.

SASSI FETHI

AN ORPHAN NIGHT

And your orphan night is on my chest,

A butterfly lives within the wind braids,

wherever sets the dusk…

I WAS

I was climbing a dream;

when I saw you…

sleeping in my wrinkles.

SASSI FETHI

USUALLY

Usually…

I embroider your face in the shape of a moon,

that has strayed from its orbit…

AND YOU ARE THE ENTIRE POEM

FOR THIS MORNING

Look well…

the clouds passing now,

I will choose one for this morning,

for your coming rains…

SASSI FETHI

AS IF I WERE

As if I were another…

in a cloud falling in a drop of water;

something will happen,

……………………….

if the shadow leaves the tree.

AND YOU ARE THE ENTIRE POEM

KNIT OF MY ISOLATION

The absence…

It's that thread feeing the dawn,

I will sew from it a knit for my isolation.

SASSI FETHI

THE DESCENDANT OF THE TREE

The fire washes its face…

to wash away the sadness of the chump,

and sings…

but the wind doesn't listen to it,

at the end, the chump forgot it is the descendant of the tree.

AND YOU ARE THE ENTIRE POEM

PAIN

I kissed her…

and I buried her lips in my pain.

SASSI FETHI

SIMPLY

Every morning the sun rises to spray the sky with light;

and with love brings a gift to the birds,

looks longer at its clock…

but the birds simply sing…

AND YOU ARE THE ENTIRE POEM

AN INVITATION

When I wrote the first poem, the stars invited

me for dinner...

SASSI FETHI

APERTURE IN THE ROOF

From aperture in the roof, I saw the night,

sleeping with a star.

I took him gently by the hand;

but my hand slept in the darkness.

ON A CHAIR

The night is sitting on a chair contemplating the moon;

nothing is as used to be this night,

only me…

as the night, I am sitting on a chair,

looking at the stars, and flirting with a cloud.

SASSI FETHI

CHILD

The moon is a parentless child;

always wandering around the sky,

but when the stars push it away,

it seeks shelter in the poem…

AND YOU ARE THE ENTIRE POEM

IS IT ENOUGH??

The leaf that fell down from the tree, is it enough
to be a love message to the wind

……. ?

SASSI FETHI

ONLY TWO CLOUDS

The sky is strangulated by crying…

the clouds have set the memories of sorrow on fire,

only two enamored clouds silently rolling the dice…

AND YOU ARE THE ENTIRE POEM

A KISS

And I stayed right near her…

with a poem that did not do much for me,

I was writing on my fingers a song,

to a cloud that won't pass…

Her night is as lost as a kiss.

SASSI FETHI

FACE OF A POEM

And your night…

Is warm as my song;

and I am overwhelmed by you as is a face of a poem.

AND YOU ARE THE ENTIRE POEM

UNDER THE RAIN

I walk under the rain…

I am unfamiliar on the sidewalk,

despite that…

I don't write anything, so that the rains don't drown.

SASSI FETHI

GIVE ME A BATON

O… evening give me a baton,

I will hit the lines of the twilight;

and push away the dusk out of my sight…

AND YOU ARE THE ENTIRE POEM

NOTHING

I wish nothing this night;

but…

a nipple and a poem.

SASSI FETHI

AS USUAL

I didn't look at your hand,

While you tore the whiteness;

I was as usual seducing a poem

……….

AND YOU ARE THE ENTIRE POEM

THE NIGHT IN A BOTTLE

Here I am writing down my pain, on the wrinkles of the whiteness,

and you…

as I know, you are filling up the night in a bottle.

SASSI FETHI

IF

If ....

a rose hid its scent,

and offered me a soft shawl, and didn't neglected my letters, if she kissed my face in the "rast " Rhyme, and faded away as the tears.

AND YOU ARE THE ENTIRE POEM

THE BOTTLE

With the first threads of the dawn;

I fill up the night in a bottle,

and while…

the light yearns for the dusk.

I smash the bottle.

SASSI FETHI

LAST TIME

Every night…

I pass by an olive tree groping the corner of the garden.

I heard it crying and telling with its leaves, what the hatchet did to it last time.

AND YOU ARE THE ENTIRE POEM

COMPASSION OF MY FINGERS

O… fairy,

the night on your palms resembles me,

then knit light …

from the compassion of my fingers.

SASSI FETHI

ALWAYS

Always…

when I wrote a poem, a cloud jumped from

its bed, to breed on the whiteness.

AND YOU ARE THE ENTIRE POEM

EYES OF CATS

When the night puts on its cover.

Worried…

I sleep under the wing of a poem;

and the eyes of cats guard me.

SASSI FETHI

UNDER MY FEET

perplexed, I go out at nights;

carrying in my pocket a scoop of stars…

I am holding the sky under my armpit

and , I fled to the mist…

A COFFEE

The night…

hidden under the eyebrows of the dusk;

it flowed slowly till, as if it were a coffee.

SASSI FETHI

TAKE ME TO YOU

Take me to you…

take me to the widely far song.

I really…

don't have grasp of my memory anymore.

AND YOU ARE THE ENTIRE POEM

DON'T ILLUMINATE THE WATER

So I am in the shades, calling out a tree,

that grows only in your eyes;

and don't illuminate light to burn the meeting…

SASSI FETHI

GIVE ME YOUR HAND

Devoured, under thrones of writing;

extend your fingers to draw the shadow,

then give me your hand…

to make the poem a prayer.

AND YOU ARE THE ENTIRE POEM

PLEASE

O….. the light,

…………………..

Please, do not denounce me.

SASSI FETHI

A MAN HOLDING UP HIS LAUGH

From the hole of the door,

I see a man holding up his laugh;

on a hook in the corner;

and wondering…:

how did the night leave his laugh hanging there

……….. ?

A MOMENT OF EMBRACE

The seed…

That fell from the pocket of the tree;

Is a moment to embrace,

planting a rose for every season.

SASSI FETHI

I DO NOT UNDERSTAND

I do not understand what happened?

mend my laugh from the night pain…

but, I am not the poet, who talked about this star.

AND YOU ARE THE ENTIRE POEM

THE STORY OF THE HATCHET

As I'm…

waking up in the morning on the voice;

of a tree;

recount to her daughter the story,

of the hatchet ….

SASSI FETHI

A WHISPER

I heard the whisper of lights

under my pillow,

how the night performed ablution in my room

………………………. ???

AND YOU ARE THE ENTIRE POEM

BETWEEN

Between…

her fingers, I learned how to write.

SASSI FETHI

SHE

She…

never says anything;

or articulated a word,

the tree that embarrassed the light.

AND YOU ARE THE ENTIRE POEM

OF ONE HOUR AGO

In my palm, a spike like a child's finger.

One hour ago, she was raving about the pigeon,

who kissed it…

SASSI FETHI

SWEETHEART

Do you know sweetheart,

that it's a glory to rescue me from the

clutches of the poem…?

all you have to do is…

take off the writing cord from its hands.

I HAVE

I have…

enough of sadness;

to make all the poems drown.

SASSI FETHI

WHOM?

O night, tell me;

Who is yearning for the twilight as much as I do?

AND YOU ARE THE ENTIRE POEM

HOW?

On that night…

the poems were sad as a candle,

and I was asking myself:

how did all this happen?

SASSI FETHI

FREMITUS

I'm still asking the absence:

did the moon sing on my balcony?

but my hand hasn't listen to the fremitus

of the night…

AND YOU ARE THE ENTIRE POEM

AND SO ARE YOU?

I am…

lonely as a strange balcony;

and all the birds do not know me,

you too your hand was hanging;

waiting for a poem that won't be coming.

SASSI FETHI

ON THE EDGE OF A POEM

And wait for me, on the edge of a poem;

to make my face wet with this light

………..

AND YOU ARE THE ENTIRE POEM

EVEN FOR JUST A MOMENT

Since the beginning of creation…

the sun has been turning in space relentlessly,

it never stopped even for one moment‹

to wash her feet; from the pains of the travel,

to wash the pain travels away.

SASSI FETHI

IN THE STATION

What if…

You were in a magical city, whose name you don't even know;

with a woman who left her suitcase in the station, what if…

you asked a waiter about the color of her coffee.

AND YOU ARE THE ENTIRE POEM

IN A POEM

This night...

while I was wandering in the skies, a star stuck on my jacket.

I laughed, and weaved it in my poem.

SASSI FETHI

SMELL OF PASSION

Do you know what excites me my darling

………………….. ??

The smell of passion in a moment of embrace.

AND YOU ARE THE ENTIRE POEM

BREEZE

As relieved, as a breeze;

She slept…

till the morning woke her up.

SASSI FETHI

THIS ECHO

What I miss in her voice…

to mend this echo.

PLEASE

Please… stay in my arms;

to make me feel the pain.

SASSI FETHI

HOW CAN I RAIN?

O… Cloud

How can I rain in your absence….?

AND YOU ARE THE ENTIRE POEM

HOW MUCH?

How much pain is enough for me

to write you?

a wonderful poem.

SASSI FETHI

All love and thanks to my friends who collaborated with me in this book…

To get in the hands of readers from all over the world

The novelist Nebiha Issi and Mustapha Bouarrouj.

AND YOU ARE THE ENTIRE POEM

POET'S BIO

Poet FETHI SASSI was born on the 1st of June 1962 in Nabeul Tunisia. He writes prose poetry and short poems. He participated in several national literary meetings. He is a member of the Tunisian Writers' Union and a member of the Literature Club at the cultural center of Sousse. His first book of poetry entitled "**A Seed of Love**" was published in the year 2010. The second entitled "***I dream …. And I sign on birds the last words*** " in 2013. The third book of poetry "***A sky for a strange bird***" was published in Egypt as well as a short poem book entitled "All the universe is only the face of my beloved".

SASSI FETHI

AND YOU ARE THE ENTIRE POEM

TABLE OF CONTENTS

FOR HER... UNIQUELY 7

ASCENT OF HER DESIRE 8

SUNSET 9

EPITAPH 10

IDEA 11

QUESTIONS MEMORY 12

PROVOCATION 13

THE SKY'S LIPS 14

THE DYNASTY OF WIND 15

A ROSE 16

EMBRACE ME 17

AN APOLOGY 18

AT THE PRESENCE OF SATAN 19

A SIN 20

A CHASE 21

A BUTTERFLY 22

IN THE ASCENT 23

SASSI FETHI

BREATHS 24

SO SHE IS 25

LONELY 26

THE TIME GALLOWS 27

STRANGE 28

WITH COFFEE 29

THE COVER OF DARKNESS 30

READER OF THE GRASS 31

THE POT OF THE TWILIGHT 32

DECREPITUDE 33

THE LIGHTNING CHILD 34

THE MISTAKES OF THE RAIN 35

TRAITOROUS 36

THE BREATHS OF THE NIGHT 37

SADNESS 38

SUNSET PHOBIA 39

STEALTH 40

THE TIDE 41

AND YOU ARE THE ENTIRE POEM

POTENTIAL PASSION 42

THE ABSENCE 43

A WHOOP'S DISTANCE 44

A COURTING 45

NEVER MIND 46

IN THE WORDS' AVENUE 47

A THREAD 48

AN ORPHAN NIGHT 49

I WAS 50

USUALLY 51

FOR THIS MORNING 52

AS IF I WERE 53

KNIT OF MY ISOLATION 54

THE DESCENDANT OF THE TREE 55

PAIN 56

SIMPLY 57

AN INVITATION 58

APERTURE IN THE ROOF 59

ON A CHAIR	60
CHILD	61
IS IT ENOUGH??	62
ONLY TWO CLOUDS	63
A KISS	64
FACE OF A POEM	65
UNDER THE RAIN	66
GIVE ME A BATON	67
NOTHING	68
AS USUAL	69
THE NIGHT IN A BOTTLE	70
IF	71
THE BOTTLE	72
LAST TIME	73
COMPASSION OF MY FINGERS	74
ALWAYS	75
EYES OF CATS	76
UNDER MY FEET	77

AND YOU ARE THE ENTIRE POEM

A COFFEE 78

TAKE ME TO YOU 79

DON'T ILLUMINATE THE WATER 80

GIVE ME YOUR HAND 81

PLEASE 82

A MAN HOLDING UP HIS LAUGH 83

A MOMENT OF EMBRACE 84

I DO NOT UNDERSTAND 85

THE STORY OF THE HATCHET 86

A WHISPER 87

BETWEEN 88

SHE 89

OF ONE HOUR AGO 90

SWEETHEART 91

I HAVE 92

WHOM? 93

HOW? 94

FREMITUS 95

SASSI FETHI

AND SO ARE YOU?	96
ON THE EDGE OF A POEM	97
EVEN FOR JUST A MOMENT	98
IN THE STATION	99
IN A POEM	100
SMELL OF PASSION	101
BREEZE	102
THIS ECHO	103
PLEASE	104
HOW CAN I RAIN?	105
HOW MUCH?	106

AND YOU ARE THE ENTIRE POEM

www.ingramcontent.com/pod-product-compliance
Lightning Source LLC
Chambersburg PA
CBHW070151080526
44586CB00015B/1935